GETTING POTTED IN THE DESERT

Marylee Pangman's

Monthly Garden Guide for Desert Pots

GETTING POTTED
IN THE DESERT

Monthly Garden Guide for Desert Pots

By Marylee Pangman

Published by
Marylee Pangman

Copyright © 2015
Marylee Pangman
Tucson, Arizona

Printed in the United States of America

First Edition

ISBN 978-0692859377

HEARTFELT THANKS!

This book would not have happened without the support of three amazing women in my life. First, my partner Laura who has always encouraged me to "go for the goal" and supported my efforts as a hard-working entrepreneur. Thank you Laura!

Next, Norma Gentry, who has a way of networking professionally and personally that leads you down the path you might not even realize you are on! Norma has served as my marketing professional, publicist, mentor and friend as well as the key editor of this book.

Then we have Laurel Islas. Without Laurel, you would not be holding this book in your hands. Her creative design and careful attention to detail pulled it all together in readiness for publishing. The heart and soul she has poured into "Getting Potted in the Desert" will be obvious as you turn each page.

And finally, many thanks to all of you who have asked over the years "Where can I find a book on everything you know about container gardening in the desert?" You are the true inspiration for "Getting Potted in the Desert". This book is for you!

Be Sure to Sign Up for the *"I Got Potted"* email list!

thepotteddesert.com/free-link/

I Got Potted Members receive:

Exclusive advanced information on all things potted

Plus Additional:

- ➢ Care recommendations
- ➢ Pictures with all plants listed
- ➢ Plant listings for each month's pictures

TABLE OF CONTENTS

Online Resource Link

www.PottedDesert.com/GettingPottedResources

Introduction

This book is for you, the transplanted desert dweller. Over time, you've probably experienced some plant disasters and right about now wish there were a guide to help you grow the kind of garden that you remember from "back home". My goal is to get you moving in the right direction so you can stop throwing your money in the compost heap!

This book will show you how to experience year-round living color with flowers, perennials, shrubs and trees all successfully flourishing in pots.

"I've been there!" Or, Why I Started Getting Potted

Growing up in upstate New York, I enjoyed bright colorful gardens. When we moved to Tucson, Arizona, our first attempt at landscaping the small back yard of our home was a dismal failure. Everything we planted died back in the winter leaving a barren setting that could rival any NY winter scene sans the snow.

While waiting for spring to come, I took the time to study desert planting. In my research, I learned about caliche, a cement-like substance which is just below the soil in this area so I knew that digging in the ground was out for me. The more I learned, the more I felt that potted gardens were the obvious answer!

Following my instincts, The Contained Gardener was conceived and I was off on a wonderful new career throughout which I was able to help many desert dwellers satisfy their need for living year-round color in their homes and gardens.

Today with more than 14 years of experience of how to best plan, plant and care for potted gardens, I am pleased to share this knowledge with you.

The Beauty of Pots

The creation of beautifully arranged plants in a container can be a work of art. Be it a combination of colorful flowers, perennials and/or annuals, a single planting, or succulents and cacti, a potted garden easily becomes a living, breathing addition to your home's outdoor living areas and an inviting welcome for your guests.

Throughout this book when I refer to pots, I am talking about containers that have an 18" or larger interior diameter, not small decorative pots which might be displayed on a table or a baker's rack.

The ease in creating container gardens offers instant gratification. Pots can be rearranged into new groupings, plantings can be easily changed and rather than back breaking shovel work, you can sit in a chair to tend them.

Know Thyself - What is your Gardening Personality?

Saver or Thrower? Whether you are a seasoned gardener or someone just getting started, I believe it is important to decide if you will want to save every ailing plant and each new baby or if you are apt to discard weaker plants and start with something fresh. People tend to fall into one of these categories.

I personally quickly discard any plants that originally cost less than $50. I will try to nurture a more expensive landscape plant as long as possible. At some point, after running their course in my potted gardens, plants must end up in my compost heap.

Sometime Slow & Steady is Best!

Planner, Doer or Enjoyer? Do you like to plan things out in advance? Or, do you tend to wing it, going to the nursery on a whim and bringing things home to figure out where they will go? You enjoy creating your gardens yourself, my advice is that you will be much more successful if you plan your garden needs in advance.

You will learn in the following chapters why this is so necessary when you are gardening in the desert. There are also professionals who will work with you to create just what you want and do a great job for you.

Plan Your Work & Work Your Plan

No Job is Too Big - Be careful with this one! If this is your attitude and you are just starting out, you may find yourself overwhelmed in spite of your best intentions. It's easy to get carried away at the nursery and leave with more containers/pots, potting soil and plants than can reasonably be planted in the same day. The new gardener often finds their plants in very poor shape after leaving them for a day or two before planting.

**The Joy of
Being Flexible**

Although it does help to be physically flexible in any gardening activity, potted gardens give us a great deal of flexibility both physically and in creating different plant environments. Except for the largest of pots and concrete planters, most can be relocated, put away when not in use or shifted to accommodate changing weather conditions.

Many of us of the "Baby Boomer" Generation enjoy change. Potted gardens fit that bill nicely. Tired of the look? Move pots in or out. Need something freshened up? Add a pot. Having a party? Shift your pots around to accommodate your space needs. When a plant needs a little tender loving care, move it out of sight while it recuperates (just don't forget to water it!).

**The Dirt on
Outdoor Areas**

Container gardens also allow you to capitalize on your home's microclimates. In desert zones, more than in those regions of the country with four seasons, we experience great fluctuations in conditions around our own property. Homes located on a wash are going to be colder on the side of the house located nearest the wash. If there is a large foliage canopy of trees or shrubs in part of your yard or near a structure these will be more protected from heat, cold and wind.

I encourage you to take the time to discover how different areas of your home vary in temperature and exposure before you venture out to the nursery to select plants for your container gardens. Depending on your latitude, sunny areas in the winter may be shady in the summer or vice versa.

Have Realistic Expectations

Before you plan your container gardens, evaluate how you live. Do you travel a lot during the summer? If so, invest in a dedicated pot irrigation line, and either enlist some help to keep your plants healthy while you're gone, or use plants that don't require a lot of water.

Garden How You Live

Are you casual or formal? I like big overflowing containers with riotous colors and luxuriant blossoms. Some people like neat, well-planned, formal containers. Some minimalists prefer to see each individual plant in a pot. Each to your own!

A Note About Vegetables and Herbs in Pots: The principles you are learning in this book about planting and growing in desert pots apply to herbs and veggies too. I will offer you some seasonal planting information and general care for your edibles, but for more guidance on growing your own harvest, refer to the resource section on my website for a list of resources.

Remember, this isn't brain surgery -- there's lots of room for error. Have fun and experiment. Whatever your lifestyle or personality you can create container gardens that will give you joy and bring beauty to your surroundings.

…and just so you know – when I talk about potted gardens in the desert climate, I am talking about large pots - not small decorative pots that might go on a table or baker's rack. What does large mean? At least 20" wide, providing a planting width of approximately 18 inches. It just goes up from there!

JANUARY

January is generally a slow month for gardening in the desert. Take advantage of this "quiet" time by planning upcoming spring chores and dreaming of your summer garden.

In the meantime, take care of your winter plants and enjoy their colors. Since it is cooler out, they will not produce as fast but any warm days will reward you with abundance!

Be Sure to Sign Up for the "I Got Potted" email list!

thepotteddesert.com/free-link/

January Checklist:
- ✓ Monitor irrigation and watering.
- ✓ Do NOT overwater.
- ✓ Maintain your fertilizing schedule. (Page 111)
- ✓ Cover tender annuals and plants when there is danger of a freeze.
- ✓ Deadhead your flowers weekly.
- ✓ Harvest veggies and herbs in the morning.

Notes:_____

_____

_____

_____

What to Plant

Flowers that will hold up well to the desert's January freezes are:

- Pansies
- Violas
- Alyssum
- Calendula
- Cyclamen (shade)
- Snapdragons
- Petunias

Snapdragons and Petunias will not flower as much during cold periods.

January Favorite

Gerbera Daisy

The Gerbera made it to my ultimate favorite list the year it survived one of our coldest winters. Before then, I reluctantly used Gerberas expecting them to only last a month or two. They can be susceptible to powdery mildew if they don't have enough air circulation and they need afternoon shade.

Gerbera Daisies produce incredibly large flowers on thick, sturdy stems. They last for a week or more in the vase, making them a favorite cut flower. In a pot on the east side of the house and with room to breathe, these lovely daisies outperform many other flowers and serve as a perennial plant.

The Potted Desert Edible Garden

Vegetables that are good for pots that can be planted in January are:

- Broccoli
- Greens (Any)
- Scallion
- Onion
- Swiss Chard
- Artichokes (Mid-Month)

Herbs to plant:

- Thyme
- Dill
- Rosemary
- Parsley
- Arugula
- Chives & Garlic Chives

Care for Potted Veggies & Herbs

It is best to harvest your herbs early in the morning before the sun gets hot. When harvesting, cut just above the first joint of tender growth - it takes the plant longer to send out new shoots from woody growth.

Dormant winter plants such as Adenium, Pachypodium, and most Euphorbia in containers should not be watered at this time. They are dormant and excess water will lead to root rot.

Potted Cacti & Succulents

Cacti in containers should be watered at least once this month. However, cacti and succulents in smaller containers may need to be watered more often as they will dry out more quickly due to the low soil volume.

Potted Rose Care: The Month of Pruning

- Do not fertilize this month.
- Continue to water your potted roses every three to four days depending on the daytime temperatures.
    - Be sure you are deep watering so the entire soil volume is wet and water comes out of the drainage hole.
    - Potted roses need to be watered more often than roses in the ground.

Pruning is the Most Important Task this Month!

- Follow these steps:
    - Remove dead, weak and crossing canes (branches) leaving only five or six canes.
    - Cut the remaining canes to 12"-18".
    - Dab any holes you see in the tops of stems with wood glue to discourage insect infestation.
    - Once pruning is complete, remove all remaining leaves (including new leaves) in order to give plants a brief time of dormancy.
    - After pruning and de-leafing roses, gather up all debris and place in the trash (not the compost heap).

- Post pruning is an ideal time for re-potting.
    - Re-potting may be needed if the soil has become too compacted to allow the tiny hair roots of the roses to get the oxygen they need.

- Plant new miniature roses so they have ample time to get established before the onset of summer heat.

SPECIAL ATTENTION THIS MONTH

Your landscaper might turn your timer off as landscape plants don't need as much water in the winter. If your pots are on a drip line, be sure that they are not turned off too. They still need regular watering.

Do not prune frost damaged plants in January!! Wait until the danger of frost is over – the average last frost date varies in the southwest depending on your elevation and locale.

Dates range from mid-January in the Palm Springs area to mid-March in Tucson and mid-April in Albuquerque. Check the online resource guide for a link to your area's date.

The exception to the "No Pruning Frost Damaged Plants" rule in January is for dormant grasses. Cut back on any you have in pots. You might also need to divide it if they have overgrown the pot.

- Monitor temperatures and protect succulents and tropical plants when the forecast calls for a freeze.

- Cover frost-tender plants with burlap, sheets or frost cloth. Do not use plastic sheets or containers to cover plants.

- Do not water succulents if the forecast calls for a freeze.

FEBRUARY

In recent years, February weather in the Southwest has become very unpredictable. Experiencing deep freezes as well as unseasonably warm spells, our plants have been confused by extreme temperature fluctuations. Extra care is needed in February.

Don't be fooled into thinking winter is over with a warm week in February. We can still expect freezing temperatures this month and even into March and April, depending on your elevation.

February Checklist:

✓ In order to keep your winter flowers blooming into May, provide them with some regular attention. Deadhead your flowers weekly. Be sure to pinch them back to the originating stem, not just the flower. This will best support continuous bloom.

✓ Fertilize your potted plants every two weeks with a water soluble fertilizer. Best applied with a hose applicator. Fertilize any potted citrus or other fruit trees (directions in following pages). Plant color annuals (see list below).

Take a regular coffee break with your garden this month so you can enjoy your blooms for months to come!

✓ Watch shallow-rooted newly planted annuals, which can quickly dry out in early spring winds.

Notes:_____

_____

_____

What to Plant

- Petunias
- Primrose
- Dianthus
- Poppy
- Stock

February Favorite **Amazon Dianthus**

I love Dianthus because it can shine from late summer to early winter when there are few bloomers available - hence my term for it as a 'shoulder season plant.'

Then along comes the '**Amazon**' Dianthus and this trusted plant now soars above the heights of other annuals with large, showy flower heads in neon cherry, purple and a deep fuchsia called rose. With a strong and long blooming season, Amazon Dianthus is truly a star.

The Potted Desert Edible Garden

Vegetables to Plant

- Get in another planting of all your cool season veggies if you have room.
  - Go ahead and transplant more greens for an early spring salad. (Spinach, all Lettuces, Mesclun, Swiss Chard, Kale)
- Plant transplants: Artichokes, Asparagus, Chard, Kohlrabi, Lettuce and Onion.
  - If you set out transplants before mid-February protect them from the cold!
- If you want to add a Tomato to your potted flower garden, you will want to keep it groomed so it can still show off.
  - Tomatoes must be transplanted early enough to develop roots, flower and set fruit before hot weather arrives, so set them out as early as mid-February in low and mid desert regions.
  - Watch for frost and cover for protection until mid-March.

Herbs to Transplant:

- Bay
- Catnip
- Chives
- Garlic Chives
- Lemon Grass
- Marjoram
- Mint (in its own pot)
- Oregano
- Sage
- Thyme
- Yarrow

Continue to harvest mature vegetables. Harvesting greens and herbs on a regular basis promotes new growth.

Care for Potted Veggies & Herbs

Fertilize fruit producing vegetables with a water-soluble fertilizer.

🌑 Pruning of roses should be completed by mid-February. See January for full instructions.

Potted Rose Care: The Month of Fertilizing

🌑 Apply both a pesticide and a fungicide to pruned roses and the ground around the plants. Fungus spores such as mildew can live through the winter in your soil.

🌑 Apply long-term or organic fertilizer, such as Max Magic Mix, Bandini Rose Food or homemade compost. Also, it helps to add superphosphate at this time since it takes a while to break down. Scratch it into the soil and water in.

🌑 Two weeks following the long-term fertilizing, begin a regular short-term fertilizing program which consists of using a water soluble fertilizer with a hose applicator according to the manufacturer's directions, every two weeks.

🌑 Once growth appears, start a hose-blasting program in the mornings to deter aphids and powdery mildew.

🌑 Continue to water roses. As daytime temperatures increase, increase watering frequency.

Potted Cacti & Succulents

If you don't get additional winter rains this month, be sure to water potted cacti and succulents. You can also fertilize them with a water soluble fertilizer. I suggest half strength in your potted plants.

SPECIAL ATTENTION THIS MONTH

Fertilize Citrus Around Valentine's Day

◉ Water both the day before and immediately after applying granular fertilizers.

◉ Use a granular fertilizer according to package directions. Size and age of the trees determine how much fertilizer you use.

Newly planted trees do not need fertilizer the first 1-2 years after planting.

◉ Fertilize mature trees away from the trunk, meaning the outer two thirds of the ground under the leaf canopy where the most active roots are.

Continue to pick your citrus. You do not need to harvest all of the fruit just because the trees are flowering. Grapefruit and Valencia Oranges will continue to sweeten on the trees.

Frosted or Frozen Plant Damage - Do not be tempted to prune back frost damaged plants yet. Wait until the danger of frost is over but BE READY to cover tender annuals in case there are more frost surprises.

MARCH

Even though local plant nurseries have many spring and summer flowers for sale this time of year, I do not recommend starting your repotting season until mid to late April, depending on your elevation.

Expecting flowers planted in March to bloom and thrive until October is an unfair request of any living thing in our harsh summer sun. In all fairness to our flowering friends, they do much better when we split the year into two growing periods and ask them to provide us with six months of beautiful blooms!

March Checklist:

✓ Check your irrigation system and be prepared to increase watering frequency as temperatures warm up.

✓ Clean up all plant debris – especially from leaf loss and cactus demise.

✓ Continue to deadhead and apply water soluble fertilizer every two weeks.

✓ Prune leggy flowers back to the center of the plant where you see new growth.

Notes:_____

_____

_____

March Favorite

Basil

Ahhhh, Basil...eat, smell and enjoy it in any of your pots that get six hours of sun. Frost tender, you may want to bring it inside to a bright window in colder months. My favorite varieties are Sweet Basil and Dark Opal Basil - both can grow 14" to 20" and do best with regular watering (not drenched).

Sweet Basil is the best choice for Italian sauces, soups and pesto. In the summer months, it does better with afternoon shade. Harvest the top four leaves often to keep the plant growing and sweetly flavored.

Dark Opal Basil adds deep color to summer floral displays and a spicy flare to a salad. The purple leaves contrast well with primary colors in pots.

What to Plant
- Geraniums (protect from frost)
- Marigolds (protect)
- Petunias
- Snapdragons
- Dianthus
- Dusty Miller

The Potted Desert Edible Garden

Great Fillers for Your Container Combinations:
- Basil (protect from frost)
- Bay
- Cuban-Oregano
- Lemon Grass
- Lemon Verbena
- Mexican Oregano
- Oregano
- Scented Geraniums
- Thyme

Care for Potted Veggies & Herbs

If your herbs have become heavy or leggy, give them a good cutback. You can safely prune them to 1/3 of their height if needed.
Be sure to continue to harvest them every week so they produce tender young growth.

Potted Cacti & Succulents

Water potted cacti and succulents once this month if there is no measurable rain.

Potted Rose Care: *Nurture, Nurture, Nurture.*

● Now is the time to begin a proper fertilization schedule, and at each step, be sure to water well the night before fertilizing.

● For the first week use an organic fertilizer, scratch into the earth and water.

● Two weeks later, use a water soluble fertilizer and repeat every two weeks.

If you have newly planted roses, DO NOT FERTILIZE them until after their first bloom!

● Use a fish emulsion once a month to help get microorganisms growing.

● Spray your Roses! Spring brings aphids, thrips, and mildew to your plants. Spray roses in the morning with a jet spray setting on the hose, twice a week to assist in preventing unwanted pests and mold.

● Continue to water roses and increase watering frequency to three times per week as the temperatures increase. Make sure to water until the water begins draining through the bottom hole.

If you have annuals planted with roses, you will need to water more frequently.

Daytime temperatures:

70' s ~ Water every 4 - 5 days

80's ~ Water every 3 - 4 days

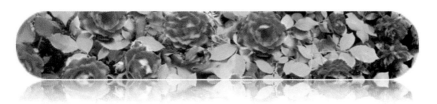

SPECIAL ATTENTION THIS MONTH

Watch for a surprise frost and cover tender annuals.

- Do not be tempted to prune back frost damaged plants yet – we need to wait until the danger of frost is over.

Potted Citrus Care

Unlike other fruit trees, you don't need to prune citrus trees on a regular basis. However, you might want to if you have frost damage, crossing or dead branches. If this is the case, prune after all danger of frost has past!

- Plant citrus after the danger of frost is past.

  - If you have not fertilized your citrus, be sure to do so now.

  - Remove any suckers growing from below the tree's graft.

  - As the potted trees grow, let the branches and foliage start as low as 12" above the soil level. The best fruit is produced on the lower two thirds of the tree so raising the skirt reduces the amount of the fruit it will produce.

- While pruning frost damaged plants, wait to prune after new growth has started.

Potted Ornamental Shrubs

- Shape ornamental shrubs so the new spring growth will fill in the bare branches and holes left from pruning.

- When you prune shrubs or perennials, do not remove more than 1/4 of the total plant.

- Always use sharp, sterile, quality pruning tools and disinfect them between cuts to prevent the spread of disease.

APRIL

By now, with proper care through the winter and spring, your potted gardens should be star performers. You still have time to enjoy them until late April or May before removing. Summer flowers planted then should last through the entire season. Waiting will give you more options at the nursery too!

However, if you just can't wait, be prepared to add some new plants in August to refresh your pots when the April plantings can no longer produce blooms or new growth.

Moving into Summer Potted Gardens

NOTE: Newly planted pots need daily water!

April Checklist:

✓ Time to check your irrigation system

✓ Review past water bills to track your usage - look for any obvious changes.

✓ Check your system for leaks.

✓ Do Not ASSUME anything - you need 1" of rain each day to be safe in turning off the irrigation for any length of time. Your pots will need water again in one to two days. Don't forget to turn it back on!

✓ Adjust irrigation timers. As temperatures increase, so do the water needs of your garden. To give plants just the right amount, start by adjusting the timer to increase the number of days per week it operates, but not the number of minutes per cycle. If your pots are not getting thoroughly wet throughout the soil volume, increase the length of time by one minute at a time.

Notes:_____
_____
_____
_____

What to Plant

At 2000-2500 feet, planting takes place in late April. Plant lower elevations in early April and higher elevations in late May.

For a complete list of plants for sun and shade, see the Appendix

Summer plant options include a wide selection of flowers and foliage plants. Some of my favorites are:

- Pentas
- Vinca
- Gaillardia (Mexican Blanket)
- Caladium (Shade)
- Angelina (Summer Snaps)
- Diamond Frost (Euphorbia)
- Coleus (Most Shade)

April Favorite

Agave 'Blue Glow'
(Attenuata x A. Ocahui 'Blue Glow')
This striking agave has deep blue-green leaves with maroon leaf margins, is hardy to 15°, and forms a 3- by 3-foot rosette. Find it at your local nurseries and be sure it is 'Blue Glow' and not 'Moon Glow.'

The Potted Desert Edible Garden

Vegetables to Plant
Eggplant and Peppers are lovely in spring pots. The fruit color and depth add to potted combinations. Purple or white eggplant with red peppers is a gorgeous combination.

Herbs to Plant

- Basil
- Bay Laurel
- Chives
- Lemon Grass
- Mint (in its own pot)
- Oregano
- Rosemary
- Sage
- Thyme

Care for Potted Veggies & Herbs

- If you haven't pruned your herb garden, now is the time to do it. For frost damaged herbs, look for new growth emerging on the lower half of the plant. Use sharp shears to cut the plant back by 1/3 to 1/2 or more, down to healthy new side shoots.

- Add new compost and water well.

- Fertilize producing vegetable gardens.

Potted Rose Care

- Establish a regular fertilizing schedule for your roses starting this month with both organic and water soluble fertilizers:

    - **Once a Month,** apply an organic rose fertilizer such as Max Magic Mix or a homemade compost (about one cup per bush the first month and ½ cup each month through October).

    - **Bi-Weekly:** Dilute water soluble fertilizer (Miracle Grow, Peters, Scotts, etc.) as the instructions state and shower onto each bush using your hose.

    - **Monthly -** Apply a dose of fish emulsion each month to the soil.

> Don't forget to water your roses thoroughly the night before you fertilize them!

Potted Rose Care (Continued)

Daytime
Temperature

Watering
Guidelines:

70's Water Every
4 to 5 Days

80's Water Every
3 - 4 Days

🌹 Take care of pests and fungi before they are a problem:

- Jet-Spraying roses with water **two times a week** will help reduce the **aphid** population. If a colony has gotten started, use Bayer Rose Spray or Safer Insecticide once a week.

- Warm weather brings the dreaded **Thrips** to attack the rose blooms and turn them brown. Using a small plastic spray bottle, spray the buds directly with insecticide as they begin to open. Do this at least **once a week.**

- Keep **Mildew** in check by using a good fungicide. Apply fungicide as a preventative for mildew **on a weekly basis,** don't wait for the problem to show up. It's harder to prevent damage once it's started.

🌹 **Water** - Your roses should be receiving **1-2 gallons of water each time you water**. This should provide water throughout the soil volume so that it comes out the drainage hole, keeping the soil moist but not soggy.

- The soil should not dry out between waterings.

🌹 **Mulch - Keep your soil moist and cool:**

- Put down 3" of mulch to keep soil from drying out during the hot days of summer ahead.

Potted Cacti & Succulents

- April is a great month to plant new cacti and succulents. They will have ample time to get established before the summer heat.

- When planting new succulents, you want the soil to be slightly moist but you do not need to water them after planting.

- Give them a week or so and if they are not out in any rain, give them a good watering once established.

- Make sure the pots have excellent drainage.

- Plant ½"-1" below the original soil line and add a layer of stone that brings it up to the soil line on the stem – not above. This keeps the plant from suffocating by keeping too much water at the stem just below the soil.

SPECIAL ATTENTION THIS MONTH

Watch out for strong winds this month. Be sure you have all your furnishings secured or in places that will not drag them into the pool or the neighbor's yard.

If weather advisories come out about gusting winds, be sure to water pots well before the wind arrives.

If you have pots that are notorious for tipping over, move them to a safer location!

MAY

The heat is coming!!!
NO doubt about it – we do live in the desert!

This really is the time to pay attention when I tell you that you need to be MINDFUL of your summer desert garden! You are going to need to adjust your water schedule based on the rising temperatures. Listen to your plants. They will tell you what they need.

Be Sure to Sign Up for the "I Got Potted" email list!

thepotteddesert.com/free-link/

May Checklist:

✓ Plant summer flowers in pots and beds

✓ Finish planting cacti & succulents

✓ Plant summer vegetables and herbs

✓ Place shade cloth over newly planted cacti & succulents to avoid sunburn

✓ Shade tomato plants

✓ Continue to increase watering and irrigation to your floral potted gardens

✓ Fertilize potted (and ground) citrus trees around Mother's Day (See February for more info.

Notes:_____
_____
_____
_____

When I give recommendations for watering, I assume that you are planting your potted flower gardens and roses in pots that are larger than 18" in diameter.

Pots that are smaller or any pot that is in full sun will need constant attention during the hot part of the year…which in the desert, is a really long stretch of time!

What to Plant

Shrubs:
- Yellow Bells
- Lantana
- Sky Flower
- Bird of Paradise Species

Perennials and Ground Covers:
- Guara
- Gazania
- Chocolate Flower
- Trailing Lantana
- White Plumbago
- Rain-Lilies

What to Plant (continued)

Summer Flowers (An extensive list can be found in the Appendix):

- Vinca
- Verbana
- Portulaca
- Purslane
- Pentas

- Celosia
- Salvia
- Gomphrena
- Zinnia

May Favorite

Diamond Frost

Euphorbia "Diamond Frost" made it to my "Favorites List" because of its tiny, delicate white flowers that soar above the lower plantings as a surprise cloud or dew drop hinting to something more. It will continue producing a brilliance of flowers all through the summer until a hard frost.

Diamond Frost requires minimal care – the flowers are very small and will quickly shrivel after flowering, leaving almost no traces of withered flowers or leaves. Do not over water this plant. Cluster with lower water annuals such as Vinca, Geraniums, Angelonia and Pentas.

The Potted Desert Edible Garden

Vegetables & Herbs to Plant - Try many of the different varieties. When you are buying transplants, you can smell and taste the leaves to see which you might prefer. Each of these listed below (including the peppers) will look great in pots with your summer flowers.

- Peppers
- Basil
- Oregano
- Tarragon
- Thyme

Care for Potted Veggies & Herbs

Be sure to provide shade for the more tender spring vegetables and herbs. If the sun burns too intensely, directly on plants, burning may result. You may need to add additional coverage as needed throughout summer.

Potted Rose Care

General Notes:

- Spray roses with a jet blast of water three times a week. This is the best proactive method to keep roses healthy.

- Add mulch if depleted from last month to keep soil from drying out.

- Dead head roses this month to continue this bloom cycle.

Fertilize:

- **Week 1 & 3** and every other week after: Use a water-soluble fertilizer with a hose applicator. Spray the rose leaves and buds and soak the soil thoroughly.

- **Week 4:** Apply a dose of fish emulsion.

Potted Rose Care (Continued)

🌹 **Pests and Fungi - Aphids, Mildew & Thrips - Oh My!:**

- **Aphids:** Use Bayer Rose Spray or Safer Insecticide once a week per bottle instructions to wipe them out.

- **Powdery Mildew:** Keep in check by using a good fungicide. It is best to use a fungicide as a preventative for mildew on a weekly basis, rather than waiting for the problem to show up. It's harder to prevent damage once it's started.

- **Thrips:** They attack the rose blooms and turn them brown. A simple way to control them is to get a small plastic spray bottle with your favorite rose spray and spray the buds directly as they are opening at least once a week.

🌹 **Water - Daytime Temperature Guidelines:**

- Continue to water roses. Suggested intervals based on 1 - 2 gallons of water per watering.

- Potted roses need **deep watering every two days when in the 80's and daily in the 90's.**

Special Note!! If you have potted annuals with your roses, they need DAILY water.

Potted Cacti & Succulents

May and June are great months to plant new cacti and succulents.

- Choose their new location appropriately with regard to sun/shade needs.
- Use cactus soil for all plants.
- Plant at least ½" shy of the soil line for room to add rock and not suffocate the plant.
- Water two weeks after planting unless the planting soil is absolutely dry.

 **SPECIAL ATTENTION THIS MONTH**

When we experience a very dry winter/spring, landscape plants may need extra help before moving into the extreme summer heat.

I cannot stress enough the need to **pay close atter..** to watering your plants this month.

- **Newly potted flowers may need twice a day watering for the first two weeks** of planting.
- All **pots in the sun will need daily watering**. Do not let the roots dry out!
- Water **potted cactus every two weeks** when there is no measurable rainfall.
- Monitor all **shade plantings** to water as needed (I suggest **every 2-4 days)**.

JUNE

On average, June is the hottest month of the year in the desert. I recommend that you make every effort to complete planting summer pots before June 1st so the flowers will have time to acclimate as the temperatures escalate from hot, to hotter and hottest!

If you are not able to meet this deadline, try planting in the early morning when temperatures are still in the low 70's or below. Check the long range weather forecast to help you decide on the best days.

June Checklist:

✓ Avoid pruning plants this month except for deadheading annuals. You will expose inner growth to sunburn.

✓ Watch for signs of water stress and sunburn

✓ Increase watering, but beware of hot hose water

✓ Water deeply and slowly.

✓ Keep up with container bi-weekly fertilizing schedule with a water-soluble fertilizer.

✓ When fertilizing, always be sure the soil is already moist.

✓ Stake taller flowers to keep them upright in summer winds.

✓ Garden in the early morning or late evening to beat the heat.

Notes:_____

_____

_____

_____

What to Plant

Although I just said not to plant this month, if you must, here are the safest bets for summer pots:

⦿ Bird of Paradise Species

⦿ Lantana   ⦿ Portulaca

⦿ Guara   ⦿ Perslane

⦿ Gazania   ⦿ Pentas

June Favorite

Golden Yucca Marginata -
Yucca Recurvifolia "Marginata."

I stumbled upon this plant in a "big box" store. Its variegated golden color caught my eye— and as a succulent, I was drawn to it as a low-water plant. I hoped that it would hold up in full sun—and that I would not have to run drip irrigation to it.

The yucca lived up to my expectations and beyond! This slow-growing beauty has become one of my favorite plants used to create a tropical effect. It does well in full sun, although as we all do, it would prefer a little afternoon respite.

It is a clean plant, requiring water every two weeks. With a deep soaking in the summer and monthly watering in the winter, it's the perfect plant for an entryway, pool area or anywhere you want something unique and relatively carefree.

The flowing soft leaves on this handsome yucca are green-centered and yellow-edged, approximately three feet in length, arching from an eventual 3-plus-foot trunk. (Remember I did say slow-growing!) Large trusses of white flowers blossom in summer.

The Potted Desert Edible Garden

Because of the intense summer heat, production of flowers decreases on some varieties of tomatoes, bell peppers and cucumbers. Some flowers may not produce fruit and eventually drop off because pollen can be damaged by temperatures over 90 degrees.

Depending on the type of tomato plant and if they survive over the summer, they should begin to produce fruit again in the fall. Some smaller tomato fruiting varieties will still continue to produce fruit through the summer months.

What to Plant

With the heat of these next two months, I would plant cautiously now. In pots that have some space, you might still try adding well grown quart or gallon size plants of peppers and perennial herbs such as oregano and thyme. Be sure to keep them nicely watered and if possible, provide them with some afternoon shade while they get established in their new home.

Vegetables:
- Eggplant
- Jerusalem Artichoke
- Jicama
- Pepper (by mid-month)
- Sweet Potato
- Tomatillo

Herbs:
- Basil (put in shade)
- Cuban-Oregano
- Mexican-Tarragon
- Mexican-Oregano

Care for Potted Veggies & Herbs

- If you are experiencing wilt in the leaves of veggies and herbs but your soil is moist, protect them with shade cloth until it cools off a little or we get a couple days of cloud cover.
- Keep the shade covering close at hand so you can easily add or remove it. Use frames to keep the cloth away from direct contact with the plants.

Potted Rose Care

Just what is early in the morning? Before sunrise - so you set the alarm or set your irrigation for before 5am!

General Notes:

- Water potted roses early in the morning every day.
- Water deeply.
- "Dead head" at least once a month.
- Apply a half strength liquid fertilizer once a month, the day after you water roses.

Pests and Fungi: Spider Mites:

- Look for dead and falling leaves; webs and/or a salt and pepper appearance on the underside of the leaves.
- Treatment - use a miticide or blast the rose bushes with a strong water spray every two to three days.

Potted Cacti & Succulents

See May Please!

SPECIAL ATTENTION THIS MONTH

- **HOT HOSE WATER!** The first water coming out of your hose will be hot during the summer months. Each time you use the hose, be sure to let all water out after turning the spigot off. Then, spray the startup water into the pool or onto a non-vegetative area until it runs cool. Watch out for the heat on the nozzle too!

- Stop mosquitoes before summer rains by eliminating places where water may collect.

- **Water, Shade and More Water - Need I say more?**

What can I say – it is July and we live in the desert where it is hot and dry. Some regions may experience the onset of monsoons which will provide our plants with a little relief – largely from the cloud cover.

Be sure to check out the special attention section this month for monsoon pre-planning!

Sign up for the *I Got Potted* email list and get exclusive information on all things potted!

thepotteddesert.com/free-link/

July Checklist:

✓ Avoid planting new plants this month unless they are cacti.

✓ Watch for signs of water stress (wilting plants) and sunburn (brown or tan blotches on leaves.) For these situations you need to increase watering (if the plants are wilting) and provide shade protection if they are getting sunburned.

✓ Water potted plants and flowers daily. Beware of hot hose water!

✓ Continue to deadhead annuals and prune to create new growth and a well-shaped plant.

✓ Fertilize potted gardens every two weeks with a water soluble fertilizer. Monsoon rains will support wild growth!

✓ Do a mosquito check to make sure you have no areas of standing water.

✓ Share your early morning coffee or tea time with your pots to make sure they are getting adequate water. If they are wilting in the early morning, you need to adjust the water duration and possibly water again in the late afternoon.

If leafy plants are wilting in the afternoon, before adding an evening watering, check to see if the soil is damp. If it is still moist, the leaves are suffering from heat wilt and do not need more water. They should recover by morning. If you feel bad for them, mist the leaves but don't water them in.

Notes:_____

_____

_____

_____

What to Plant

Let's take this month off from planting. We want success for both our plants and ourselves. No heat stroke allowed!

July Favorite

Summer Snaps Angelonia

Summer Snap Dragons are among my favorite flowers to use this season. I am always looking for a tall flowering plant for my desert potted gardens AND one that will last the entire summer. Summer Snaps or Angelonia Angustifolia fit that bill perfectly. In this photo, summer snaps are planted with white Profusion Zinnias and Trailing Scaevola. They are rapidly trying to take over a "Silver King" Euonymus shrub which will take the shade they provide just fine.

The Potted Desert Edible Garden

- **Keep plants moist.** Wilted leaves in the morning are a sign of too little water or root bound pots. Late afternoon wilting may be heat stress and plants will respond well to a water mist.

- Be sure to check the soil before adding more water. Do not overwater!

- Prune back tomatoes by two-thirds to encourage new growth and set fruit for fall.

Care for Potted Veggies & Herbs

- Continue to harvest mature vegetables. Harvesting greens and herbs on a regular basis promotes new growth.

- Fertilize fruit producing vegetables with a water-soluble fertilizer.

Potted Rose Care

General Notes:

- Water early in the morning. Potted roses need to be **watered daily.** Deeply water to encourage roots to grow to where the soil is cooler.

- **Deadhead** roses but leave all old leaves and canes to help shade the plant.

- **Do not fertilize** roses this month.

Potted Cacti & Succulents

- If you don't get any rain this month, water your potted cactus deeply.
- Small pots should be checked every two weeks to make sure the soil has not completely dried out.

Too often homeowners make the mistake in thinking that a monsoon storm means they can cut back on irrigation or hand watering for their pots, gardens and other plants. Points to consider:

- It has to rain at least one inch in order to saturate the root ball of your plants (get yourself a rain gauge so you know how much rain your yard has received)

- Pots under a ramada, tree or overhang do not receive enough (if any) rain.

- A deep soaking rain (more than 1") received over a long period of time, like several hours, will only replace one day's worth of watering.

- A missed watering will cause your plants to be stressed and this invites problems including pest invasion and disease.

- Be sure to batten down all the hatches - i.e. watch for tipping pots, furniture and anything else that can blow over!

AUGUST

We have made it to August and as the sun rises a little later each morning, we can try to coast into September.

This month's list will be on the short side. Your most important tasks are listed in the Special Attention section for this month as heat and monsoons are our chief concerns...that and **staying cool and hydrated!**

August Checklist :

✓ Trim and dead-head spent flowers.
✓ Water potted plants and flowers daily. Beware of hot hose water!
✓ Fertilize potted gardens every two weeks with a water soluble fertilizer. Monsoon rains will support wild growth!
✓ Check for signs of water stress and sunburn
✓ Check for standing water in saucers and other mosquito gathering places.

Notes:_____

_____

_____

_____

What to Plant

If you have some annuals that are struggling, check out your nursery to see if they have a late summer supply of well grown replacements. If they do, grab some and fill in any holes caused by tired plants. Plants to look for include:

◉ Pentas
◉ Vinca
◉ Summer Snaps (Angelonia)

Keep your money out of the compost heap! Do not be tempted by the less expensive six packs or jumbo packs of annuals. Their root systems do not have enough soil volume to protect them from the sudden heat exposure they will experience once they leave the nursery. Use 4", quart or gallon plants.

I do not recommend using plants in pots that go dormant in the winter or need to be pruned each winter. Plants such as Grasses and Salvias fall into this category and although they are beautiful during the hot months, they do not do our pots justice during the winter months. Additionally, other plants such as Bougainvillea, Sages and Texas Rangers which are great in our landscape, do not perform well in pots. They need room to spread their roots much further than a pot will allow.

August Favorite

Gopher Plant

Staying away from high water flowers and shrubs, we can create beautiful pots with many cacti and succulents. If we are aiming for lushness, there is nothing better than the Gopher Plant. Keeping it well groomed as lower branches brown up makes it a very satisfying plant year round. (Note, the plant pictured is in full spring bloom!)

The Potted Desert Edible Garden

Be on the lookout for grubs this month. If you have a plant that is suddenly dying without any apparent explanation, grubs could be the culprit. They are large, fat worms burrowed deep in the soil. You can treat for grubs with the insecticide Sevin.

Care for Potted Veggies & Herbs

- Keep edible plants well hydrated.
- Shade with no more than a 50% shade cloth.
- Harvest vegetables and herbs regularly.

Potted Cacti & Succulents

- Since you probably watered cacti and succulents last month, wait to see if you get some August or monsoon rains. As long as the pots are out where they can catch the rain, they should be good to go.
- Without rain, water again this month.

Potted Rose Care

- **General Notes:**
- **Water early** in the morning daily.
- **Deeply** water to encourage roots to grow to where the soil is cooler.
- **Deadhead** roses but leave all old leaves and canes to help shade the plant.
- **Do not fertilize** roses this month.

 **SPECIAL ATTENTION THIS MONTH**

Please take a second and flip back to July's notes for this area as well as what is listed below!

- ⦿ Be sure to batten down all the hatches! Monsoon rains can mean heavy winds.
- ⦿ Watch for tipping pots, furniture and anything else that can blow over, off a shelf or ledge, into your pool or even your neighbor's yard!

SEPTEMBER

As we move into September, I ask you – "How are you using your patio?" I know mine has gone largely unused during these hot days but I am chomping at the bit to sit outside, enjoy our outdoor living room and get as many "last" days in our pool that I can.

Unless we are blessed with some late monsoons, make sure landscape plants are getting enough water. A morning watering schedule should be adequate for your potted gardens. By now, mature plants should provide your soil with shade and should not need a second watering later in the day. If you see afternoon wilt, be mindful if plants actually need more water or just cooler temperatures!

Falling **for Your Potted Garden!**

September is heavy with "To Do's" for Desert Dwellers. Plan the month so you are not trying to accomplish it all in one weekend allowing time for you to enjoy your fall garden and other early fall activities!

NOTE: Newly planted pots need daily water!

SPECIAL CITRUS NOTE: Be careful fertilizing potted citrus IF you have summer flowers planted around your tree. The heavy dose of fertilizer can be deadly to the annuals. You might wait until you are planning to remove the plants if you are not willing to take the risk. If you have been fertilizing your citrus tree pot with the bi-weekly water soluble fertilizer, it will not hurt to wait.

September Checklist:

- **Fertilize** citrus this month (See February for more details).

  - Read the instructions on the package for more information.

  - Use Ammonium Sulfate, Ammonium Phosphate or Citrus Food fertilizer.

  - The amount of fertilizer needed per year depends on the age, the size, and the type of tree.

  - Be sure to fertilize out to the same diameter as the tree's canopy.

- Light **pruning** of roses is important this month. See below for details.

- As temps cool down, reduce the frequency of your irrigation to your pots.

- Continue to **deadhead** annuals and prune to create new growth and a well-shaped plant.

- **Feed** potted gardens every two weeks with a water soluble fertilizer. Follow the directions on the label.

September 's Checklist (Continued)

- Jet Spray all potted plants including flowers, shrubs, cacti, succulents - All of them, every day if you are able.

  - This increases air circulation and deters pests and disease (like spider mites, powdery mildew, aphids, etc.).

  - Do this in the early morning.

  Notes:_____

  _____

  _____

  _____

What to Plant

This month, it is best to plant flowers that I call shoulder season flowers, many of which will do well all winter long. Be sure to plant in the early morning and make sure the plants are well hydrated before you plant. Then water them thoroughly after planting. These include:

- Bacopa
- Dianthus
- Geraniums
- Osterspermums
- Petunias
- Snapdragons

*September
Favorite*

Scaevola

Scaevola is a gorgeous cascading plant, also known as a "Fan" flower. It is a durable flower that takes the heat without wilting and produces an abundance of lavender-blue or white blooms all summer. It's great in sunny pots and as a perennial during the desert's mild winters - it will often perform all year around!

The Potted
Desert Edible
Garden

Vegetables to Plant: :

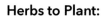

- All Leaf Greens
- Beets
- Broccoli
- Carrots
- Peas
- Radish
- Turnips
- Swiss Chard

Late in the month transplants:

- Celery
- Chard
- Lettuce
- Onions
- Strawberries
- Tomatoes

Herbs to Plant:

- Chives
- Cilantro
- Cumin
- Dill
- Fennel
- Marjoram
- Mint
- Oregano
- Parsley
- Rosemary
- Thyme

Remember to always keep mint at bay by growing it in its own pot!

Care for Potted Veggies & Herbs

- Cut back summer tomatoes to gain new growth and spur flowering.
- Monitor water needs based on temperatures.

Potted Cacti & Succulents

- Depending on how much it has rained in your area this month, you may need to water potted cacti.
- The best plan is to test the soil and see if it is damp. If it is, then wait until it dries out before watering. If it is dry now - go ahead and give it a soaking.
- When you do water, give it a half strength dose of the same water soluble fertilizer you use on other potted plants.

Potted Rose Care: Busy Hands!

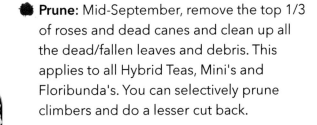

Prune: Mid-September, remove the top 1/3 of roses and dead canes and clean up all the dead/fallen leaves and debris. This applies to all Hybrid Teas, Mini's and Floribunda's. You can selectively prune climbers and do a lesser cut back.

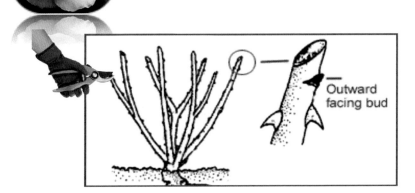

Outward facing bud

Potted Rose Care (Continued)

Water roses well before and after fertilizing!

Don't try to jump start your roses by giving them a big boost of fertilizer when it is still over 90 degrees. When it starts to cool down at night (temps in the 60's), apply full strength fertilizer.

● **Water:** Deeply water to encourage roots to grow to where the soil is cooler.

- Roses in pots need daily water.

- Never let them dry out or the soil will become hard to re-hydrate.

- Check your irrigation system often.

● **Feed:** If the weather continues to be hot, only apply organic fertilizer like Max Magic Mix, Mills Magic Mix, Hickman's compost etc. or a half strength liquid fertilizer.

● Give roses their fall dose of **Epsom Salts**. Use one half cup per standard rose bush and ¼ cup per miniature rose bush.

● **Pests:** Unless you have a bad case of bugs or mildew, don't start weekly spraying for pests and mildew until early October. Spider mites are still a possibility, so continue to blast roses with your water wand two or three times a week.

⚠ **SPECIAL ATTENTION THIS MONTH**

Go back to the 'To Do' sections. Don't miss these September tasks:

◉ Fertilize Citrus Trees

◉ Prune back roses and start your fertilizing program.

OCTOBER

This time of year presents us with quite the conundrum. With temperatures in the 80 - 95+ range it still is a little too early to plant winter flowers with any long-lived success and yet you will find local nurseries overflowing with them! I'm sure you are tired of your summer flowers (and they for sure are tired themselves), but to save you the agony of losing new plants before their time, please wait, wait, wait!!!

I can guarantee you that temps will rise again for our own version of "Indian Summer." Therefore to enjoy a potted garden that is absolute instant gratification, wait until the third or fourth week of the month!

October Checklist:

- Continue to deadhead annuals and prune to create new growth and a well-shaped plant.
- Feed potted gardens every two weeks with a water soluble fertilizer. Follow the directions on the label.
- Jet Spray all potted plants including flowers, shrubs, cacti, succulents - All of them, every day if you are able.
  Notes:_____
  _____
  _____
  _____

What to Plant

The ideal time for planting winter plants (both flowering plants and vegetables) is when the night time temperatures are consistently in the low 60's or 50's, especially for delicate plants like Pansies and Violas.

I want your winter flowers to last at least until next May which is 6 - 7 months away. Trying to get any more out of them is asking a lot! If you just can't wait, start with heartier plants ('shoulder plants') that can cross over seasons:

- Dianthus
- Petunias
- Snap Dragons
- Sweet Pea seeds at end of the month for late winter blooms.
- Winter Annuals Galore – See list in Appendix.

October Favorite *Silver Dust Artemisia* is grown-up Dusty Miller. Similar in color and leaf structure, Silver dust is

actually a perennial that puts up a pale lavender flower with soft foliage. It can also be mistaken by an untrained eye, as an artichoke. All plants in this family are low water, easy growers that respond well to pruning and have a certain scent, not unpleasant to humans, but that javelina, rabbits and deer do not like.

The Potted Desert Edible Garden

It's time to begin fall planting! Add lots of fresh compost to beds in addition to organic fertilizers like bat guano, fish meal, cotton seed meal and even a little Epsom salts. If using pots, be sure to dedicate this kind of mix only to veggie gardens as it will be too rich for flowers.

Veggies to Plant:
- Broccoli
- Brussel sprouts
- Cabbage
- Cauliflower
- Celery

If you have large pots (24"+), you can plant the following, making sure you do not crowd the individual plants:
- Radish Seeds every ten to fifteen days for a continuous harvest.
- Lettuce Seeds every two to three weeks for continual salad basics.

The Potted Desert Edible Garden (Continued)

Herbs to Plant (Early in the Month):

- Cilantro
- Dill both
- Parsley
- Garlic
- Chamomile

Care for Potted Veggies & Herbs

- Keep newly planted herbs and vegetables well watered.
- Never let the soil dry out completely.

Potted Rose Care

- **Water:** Deeply water to encourage roots to grow to where the soil is cooler.

  - Deep water every other day. Rose bushes should continue to bloom until the first heavy frost.

  - Never let them dry out or the soil will become hard to re-hydrate.

  - Check your irrigation system often.

- **Feed:** Start bi-weekly liquid fertilizing program if you have not already.

- **Deadhead**: Continually deadhead roses down to an outward facing 5-leaf.

- Rose Pests:

  - Keep an eye out for powdery mildew. At first signs, spray with a fungicide or wash (jet spray) roses with water daily.

  - Spider mites are still a possibility, so continue to blast roses with your water wand two or three times a week.

Potted Cacti & Succulents

- Test the soil and see if it is damp. If it is, then wait until it dries out before watering. If it is dry now - go ahead and give it a soaking.
- When you do water, use a half strength dose of the same water soluble fertilizer used on your other potted plants.

SPECIAL ATTENTION THIS MONTH

I don't mean to harp, but please heed my caution of planting winter annuals too early; especially Pansies, Violas, and Ornamental Kale.

The kale will bolt early and you will be faced with filling huge holes in your pots in March.

Intense heat can cause plants like Pansies and Violas to weaken and become stretched in appearance. If they don't succumb to heat stress, they will not be as hearty as needed to thrive all winter.

Remember, I am continually trying to keep your money out of the compost heap!

NOVEMBER

Now is the time to begin planning for frost events. Historically, the average first freeze in the middle desert occurs around November 15. Purchase and/or stage your frost protection so that if and when an event happens, you are prepared.

Use fabric such as burlap or old sheets; never use plastic as it causes plants to burn where they come into contact. Frost cloth can be purchased at garden centers.

November Checklist:

Plant winter flower gardens this month to your heart's content. With the cooler temperatures on the way (at last), be sure to make the following adjustments:

✓ Reduce the frequency of watering schedule for your landscape plants.

✓ Water potted plants only once a day.

✓ All watering should be done in the morning after the sun is up.

✓ Only fertilize container plants. Other plants are now going into their dormant periods and if you push new growth with fertilizer you risk frost damage to the new tips.

✓ Begin checking the forecast for freeze warnings

✓ Prepare to cover and protect sensitive plants when temperatures drop below 28°F, tropicals at 34°F.

✓ Bring potted plants, including succulents indoors when in doubt about cold sensitivity.

Notes:_____

_____

_____

_____

What to Plant

All winter annuals such as Alyssum, Pansy, Viola, Dianthus, Petunia, Snapdragons, Stock. See complete list in the Bonus section.

November Favorite

Heuchera

Grown as a foliage plant, Heuchera or Coral Bells has come a long way through a multitude of hybridizing. The array of leaf colors is amazing and striking. From the traditional coppery shades to black to chartreuse, if you see a low-lying, leafy plant in a garden that just grabs your attention, you can bet it is a Heuchera. I recently discovered these are also critter resistant. Best planted in the fall after temperatures subside, Heuchera can handle winter morning sun and summer shade. It might give up in the full-on hot summer days, but cut it back and plant some protecting plants around it, it may regrow in the fall.

The Potted Desert Edible Garden

Vegetables to Plant:

- Broccoli
- Brussel Sprouts
- Cabbage
- Carrot
- Cauliflower
- Lettuces
- Mustard Greens
- Radish
- Spinach
- Swiss Chard (*also provid cool season color*)

The Potted Desert Edible Garden (Continued)

Flower Edibles to Plant:
- Calendula
- Nasturtiums
- Pansies
- Violas

- **Herbs to Plant:**
- Cilantro
- Parsley
- 'Tuscan Blue' Upright Rosemary (Rosmarinus Officinalis 'Tuscan Blue')

Potted Rose Care

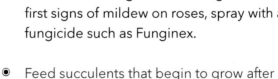

- Now that temperatures are cooling down, you can begin to decrease the frequency of watering - not the amount.
- Continue fertilizing until fall bloom shows are over, and gradually decrease fertilizing towards the end of November to discourage any new growth and give the roses a brief rest period.
- Keep a watchful eye for powdery mildew. As the nighttime temperatures cool off, the conditions are right for this fungus. At the first signs of mildew on roses, spray with a fungicide such as Funginex.

Potted Cacti & Succulents

- Feed succulents that begin to grow after summer dormancy.
- Give those in containers a half- strength dose of fertilizer.

SPECIAL ATTENTION THIS MONTH

Preparing for Winter Cold

To help avoid frost and freeze damage this winter there are some important steps to take:

- Keep plants well watered. Frost will draw moisture from your plants leaves; well watered plants will experience less severe damage if they are not already dehydrated.
- Use jumbo Styrofoam cups on columnar cactus tips.
- Do not cut back frost damaged branches until March!!

Reduce Heat Loss:

- Completely cover plants with cloth or paper (not plastic or towels!) from the top all the way to the bottom for insulation. Do not allow openings for heat to escape. This will protect down to temperatures in the 20's and 30's.
- When covering potted plants, wrap the cloth around the plant and tuck the ends into the soil area of the pot.
- Use clothespins to help hold cloth in place.

When covering your plants, do not gather the draped cloth around the trunk of the tree! Your plant is collecting heat from the soil and if it's gathered on the trunk, the warm air rising from the soil will not reach the fragile leaves.

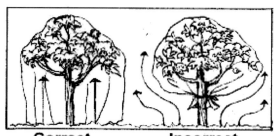

Correct   **Incorrect**

SPECIAL ATTENTION THIS MONTH (Continued)

- Remove the coverings in the morning when temperatures are around 50 degrees.
- Wrap the trunks of <u>young</u> trees to prevent damage to young, vital stem areas. This wrap can be left on all winter.

Add Heat:
- Walls and benches collect heat during the day and are good sources of heat at night.
- 100w light bulbs can provide heat to coverage plants. Hang them below the foliage, away from trunks and branches that are susceptible to burning.
- Apply a trickle of running water to the ground at the base of the tree. When water is cooled, energy in the form of heat is released.

Be mindful that not only are plants susceptible to the cold, but pipes and backflow valves can also be at risk:

- In temperate climates such as ours, pipes are often installed outside, exposed to the elements.
- When temperatures are flirting with freezing it is important that these pipes are insulated by using foam, insulation tape, and "insulation blankets"

DECEMBER

You can still plant flowers in pots for the winter. Plant when the temperatures for the week will be in the upper 70's through 80's.

Shop for the best selections at your local nurseries.

December Checklist:

✓ Snip petunias to encourage them to branch and spread and reduce the stickiness of maturing plants. Prune long stems by at least half their length and to new growth to encourage side branching.

✓ Remove the old blooms from geranium, cyclamen, calendula and other winter flowers as they fade, by cutting them off with sharp scissors or hand pruners. This will also increase flower production.

✓ Use a bi-weekly spray application of a water soluble fertilizer on all flowering plants to encourage growth and a continual show of flowers.

Notes:_____

_____

_____

_____

What to Plant

◉ Continue to plant winter annuals as mentioned in November. Feel free to keep planting them into March.

◉ Plant successive plantings of lettuce, spinach, chard, and other fast-maturing winter greens.

December
Favorite

Cyclamen

If you, like many desert gardeners, are looking for a flowering shade plant for the desert's winter months, Cyclamen is an outstanding, showy, reliable plant that will shine above any companion plant, even in deep shade. With rounded deep green leaves or variegated with silver tones, Cyclamen comes in a true red, pinks and white.

The perky flower sits above the leaves and as long as they are planted high enough and not overwatered, they will flower all winter long. When the weather gets warm, pull back even more on the water and enjoy the foliage until the fall.

When I say to plant it "high," I am referring to a flat ball like structure known as a tuber on the Cyclamen plant. This should rest above the soil level allowing it to remain somewhat 'high and dry' and be able to breathe.

The Potted
Desert Edible
Garden

Vegetable to Plant:.
◉ Successive Plantings of Head and Leaf Lettuces, Cabbage, Spinach, Chard & Other Fast Maturing Winter Greens

The Potted Desert Edible Garden (Continued)

Herbs to Plant

- Chamomile (German & Roman)
- Feverfew
- Pennyroyal
- French Sorrel

Edible Flowers - Continue to plant from last month's list.

Care for Potted Veggies & Herbs

- The best thing you can do for your vegetables and herbs this month is to **harvest them.**
- Make sure they have enough water without over-watering them in the cooler month.

Potted Rose Care

- Water potted roses two to three times each week.
- If you purchased bare root roses and have planted them in pots, it is best to move them to a protected area if the weather gets below freezing. All established roses that are in the ground require no winter protection in AZ.
- Begin now to plan for roses that will need replacing or relocating.
- Pruning needs to be completed by Feb 10, so enjoy a month of relaxation until then!

SPECIAL ATTENTION THIS MONTH

- Check your weather forecast for FREEZE WARNINGS!
- Cover the tips of sensitive columnar cacti with styrofoam cups.
- Use frost cloth or a blanket to cover aloes, citrus, and other sensitive plants when temperatures drop below 28°F.

PLANNING A GARDEN WITH POTS

Before You Think About Going Shopping - If you are starting with one pot, several or a large number, you want to have a plan before you go shopping. This will assure your success from day one.

How do you create outdoor living spaces you can enjoy?

Begin with a Walk Around - Write down areas in your outside spaces and make notes about special needs and places you want to add interest. Here is a sample listing to get you started:

- ☐ **Front Door/Entry** – I would love to create an area of color and interest at the entrance of my home.
- ☐ **Outside a Patio Door or Window** - I want to enhance the view that I see from my favorite chair
- ☐ **A Prominent but "Dead" Corner that Just Begs for Living Color** - Something that draws my attention every time I step outside
- ☐ **Patio** - I would like to create an appealing grouping on my patio that will define and soften the look of the seating area.
- ☐ **Swimming Pool** - I would like to see groupings of pots around the pool decking to create a pop of color contrast to my desert landscaping.
- ☐ **A Special Outdoor Area** - Where a single pot makes a statement and serves as a true design element and focal point.

Perhaps There is a Distinct Purpose for a "Space"

☐ **Screening:** Do you want to hide an air conditioner, pool pump or something unsightly?

☐ **Privacy:** Do you have a neighbor who can see into your yard or their house wall glares at you?

☐ **Inviting:** Do you want a more relaxed sitting area or inviting dining area?

☐ **Relaxing:** Do you want that quiet hidden space for a brief moment of your own?

Using Containers as Elements of Design – Pots, while being beautiful in their own right, can also serve the purposes listed above, but a pot or collection of pots can also be used to:

☐ Define different areas of a patio or exterior wall to break up space.

☐ Soften hard edges of square corners, like the end of seat walls, a barbecue area or steps.

☐ Mark the beginning or end of a stairway and indicate a change in a walkway. Pots can be used to create visual and structural barriers on the edge of a patio that has a drop-off.

☐ Subtly direct guests along a walkway to an entrance that might be partially hidden.

☐ Place around other areas of a home along pathways to keep interest flowing to the final destination.

Think About "The Flow"

Consider traffic patterns carefully before placing pots. Will any walkways be blocked? Can anything be moved to accommodate the pots and make the space work better? Plan ahead to be able to reposition the pots if you expect to add new furnishings or decor later. Will the pot itself be the focal point or part of a larger picture?

I recommend that you start with just one area so it does not get too overwhelming. To get a good perspective, take a look at the area where you plan to add pots, from your home and different areas of your yard to see how it will appear to you and your guests.

Often we use pots to lead the eye to a specific view. The goal here is for all items in the view to work together well. Don't place a taller pot in a place that will dominate the view unless that is your goal. If the pot is short, the eye will stop there unless there is something behind it that is slightly taller. You might consider using a broad low-bowl pot in front of a pool so that the eye can be directed to look beyond to a mountain view or other focus point.

Think About What Look You Are Going For

What should I do with my favorite small pots?

How about gathering them all up and arranging a selection of them tastefully on a baker's rack or outside sofa table in a shady spot. Plant each with individual succulents or herbs which will do just fine for a very long time. Remember – less is more. Make each pot an individual statement-not a clutter of leftovers.

Planning for Your Desert Environment

Before you finalize your plans for pot selection and placement, use the following guidelines to consider what plants you might like:

- ◉ I love color – I only want flowering plants.
- ◉ Succulents are my thing – I just cannot get enough of them.
- ◉ I prefer low water plants
- ◉ I do not want to worry about watering pots. I will add irrigation to them.
- ◉ I like the idea of a blend of succulents and flowering plants.
- ◉ I really want mostly specimen sized plants.
- ◉ I want to plant herbs and vegetables.

Using the statements from the previous page as a guideline to clarify your preferences will be very helpful in the planning process. You should have a good idea of what look, style and types of plants you prefer before you select the pots and begin creating your container garden(s).

A Short Lesson on Our Seasonal Climate and Sun Shifts

The desert climate changes from daytime temperatures of 100+ in the summer to nights of 25-30 degrees in the winter. When selecting plants you will need to consider these extreme variations.

As our sun shifts from a southern angle in the winter, moving northerly, plants that were getting a lot of southern sun will not get as much sun in the summer.

Conversely, plantings on the more northern side of the house, while in complete shade in the winter can be scorched by the hot summer sun. This is a major concern for permanent plantings in pots.

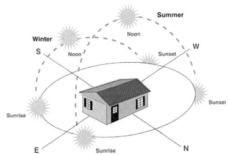

However, if you are planning to use annuals for constant color (which I wholeheartedly recommend), the sun shift will not matter because you will change out your flowers as the seasons change.

If you are totally into planning, it might be helpful to take pictures of the various areas of the yards surrounding your home, at different times of the day. You can record the sun's movement by taking photos of the shadows on your plants three times a day over the course of the four seasons.

Yes, –even though we sometimes feel that we only experience hot or cold weather, the desert really does have four seasons. These pictorial records can go far in helping you plan and not have to rely on your memory.

Exceptions - Shade | Succulents | Winter

Differently shaped pots work for many different plants. However, there are some tricks of the trade that you will want to learn so that when it is time to transplant, you can actually remove the plants from their container. Refer to the Pot Shape Chart on page 81.

Selecting pots and plants and deciding which comes first in your planning process is very much like the chicken or the egg. Considering the scale of the area where the pots will be placed, I like to choose the pots first, while keeping in mind what type of plants I want to plant in them. However, if you already have a plant in mind, you will need to select a pot based on the growing habits of that plant.

CHOOSING THE PERFECT POT

Now It's Time to Go Shopping! Bring your tape measure and your notes. It might be helpful to bring a photo of the space as well as your camera to take shots of pots you may be interested in. A good nursery or pot store will be happy to work with you and will allow you to return the pot if it does not work once you get it home. You are making an investment and they want to be sure you are happy with your selection!

> "We make rules when we try to help people succeed. However, in the world of gardening, there are exceptions to every rule!"
> *Marylee*

Size Matters More Than Looks!

When I visit with prospective clients, what I encounter most are various collections of undersized pots that they have accumulated over time and that they are very attached to. Besides being difficult to work with, these pots are usually too small and create the wrong proportions for the areas in which they are to be used. It's like using a very small end table next to a large overstuffed sofa.

Rule #1: The Bigger the Better! Buy the biggest pot that you can afford that best fits the space where you want your container garden to grow.

Rule #2: For any pot placed in the sun, select one that the top diameter is at least 18inches. Anything less than that is going to cause problems. Don't be seduced into buying something esthetically pleasing but impractical. Unless you are going to plant a cactus in it, it's not going to keep the soil cool enough for soft plantings.

You can use many types of containers for your potted garden.

Type of Pot	Comments
Concrete	**Pros**: Reliable, hold moisture well, long-lasting **Cons**: Very heavy to move if they are to be relocated; some can look very industrial
Euro-Asia Clay/Firing – i.e. Overburn Pots, Rustic Glazed Pots, Glazed Pots	**Pros**: Beautiful and varied in style, glazing and finishes, hold moisture well, long-lasting **Cons**: One of the more expensive types of pots
Metal	**Pros**: Lightweight, work in contemporary design **Cons**: Need insulation to protect soil from intense heat, may rust
Mexican and Italian Clay– i.e. Terra Cotta	**Pros**: Inexpensive, many varieties for southwest or Mediterranean décor: Try to purchase those that are high-fired. (most Mexican pottery is not high-fired except Talavera) **Cons**: Will not last as long as glazed or concrete pots; more porous; need to be sealed; dry out faster
Nursery Cans	**Pros**: Virtually Free **Cons**: NOT RECOMMENDED for long term use. Hot, not large enough for most plantings long-term.
Polypropylene ("Foam" Lightweight Pots)	**Pros**: Less expensive, many varieties, easy to carry and move around. **Cons**: Do not come with holes – easily added. Be sure they are a thick wall all the way down the pot. Otherwise it is similar to plastic.
Talavera	**Pros**: Glazed inside and out with unique southwest/ Mexican designs **Cons**: Consider not using in all day sun. Know what you are buying. Some Talavera is painted on, not fired on.

Notice that there are no plastic pots on the list on the previous page. Even though they are relatively inexpensive, these thin walled pots will not hold up to the sun and they do not belong in your container gardens. Use them for sick plants or propagating if you must, but you have spent a great deal of time and effort planning your container gardens and should use the best product you can afford.

My personal preference is for glazed pots. They have become very accessible in the last ten years. Since they are glazed, they are high-fired (fired at high temperatures) which will increase their life expectancy tenfold.

Scale and Perspective

At this stage, having the assistance of a friend would be very helpful. Give them a tape measure and have them stand where you want to place the pot(s). Position yourself in the place where you will see the pot(s) most often. Consider anything that the pot may be placed next to i.e. a column, barbecue, seating arrangement, shrub, etc. From your vantage point, look to see what size would be pleasing to your eye. Have your assistant extend the tape measure vertically to get a visual estimate of the appropriate container height and make sure it is in proportion to the surrounding area.

Once you have determined the height, have your friend stand where the pot is to be placed and extend the tape measure in front of them to find a width that fills the space nicely. Once you give them the okay, write down the measurements.

You may ultimately adjust the final selection once you go shopping for your pot, but now you have target measurements to work with. Most people tend to purchase pots that are too small - don't be afraid to go for one larger than you think you need.

Pot Shapes

Shape	Picture	Recommended Uses	Comments
Bowl with Wide Bases		All uses	The most reliable shape for windy or critter areas.
Low-Bowl		Great for a winter bowl of flowers or a year-round cactus garden	Be sure your selected plant does not need a deeper root depth.
Vase (Tall)		Gives nice height for walls and corners.	Be sure it is protected from the wind.
V or Egg Shaped (Mid-Height)		Beautiful pots, many uses	Easily knocked over by javelina or other creatures. Even wind can blow it over if it has a tall shrub or tree in it.
Urn Shapes		Annuals, small perennials	Be careful leaving well-rooted plants in for a long time. The only way to remove them may be breaking the pot.

CHOOSING THE BEST PLANTS FOR YOUR DESERT CLIMATE

Sun vs. Shade

- Place plants with similar sun/shade needs together in your pot. This will keep them all happy.
- Your local nursery will have plants arranged according to where they do best (i.e. full sun, part sun or shade). Always ask for assistance if you need help selecting the appropriate plants for your container garden.
- Be sure to watch where the nursery places the plants. Is it filtered sun, full sun or heavy shade? Do they get afternoon shade? A good nursery will show off the plants where they do best!
- Remember the sun shifts through the year. A plant placed in the shade in winter may be in full sun in the summer (or vice versa)!

Choose Plants with Similar Watering Needs

- It's also important to use plants in your container gardens with similar water requirements. Planting a high water use plant with a low water use plant is a sure way to lose one of them.
- Do rely on nursery professionals to guide you in your plant selection. Because there are many variables among annuals such as how much water they need and if they tolerate water on their leaves or flowers, make it your business to gather as much information as you can before making your purchase.

Choose Plants Proportionate to the Size of the Container

- Make sure to consider the proportion of plants to the container. A large container planted with short plants can look stunted; and a small pot with large plants is a disaster waiting to happen.

- Avoid a tall, full plant in a tall narrow based pot if placing it in the elements such as wind. The tipping risk on this combination is huge! Although they will look nice together, this combination is best in a protected courtyard or patio.

- If a plant is listed as a fast grower, be sure you consider that when selecting the pot size. You do not want to have to upsize a pot in six months. A good example is the 'Octopus' Agave. Placed in a shallow bow – while it looks

good – it will push itself out of the pot as the roots work to grow deeper in the shallow soil volume. Select a plant that has a similar look without the need to change it out so fast; such as the Agave 'Americana,' 'Artichoke' or 'Cabbage.'

Choose Healthy Plants

- Buying your plants at a reputable local nursery is a good place to start in your quest for healthy plants. You have a greater chance of getting plants that are disease and pest free and well cared for than at many big box stores. At a local nursery, you can be assured of getting a wealth of information and advice from knowledgeable staff. Do not be afraid to ask someone to help you pick out a good plant. (Get the theme here? Ask for help)!)

- Observe the **quality** of nursery. On each visit, get an overall idea of how healthy the plants look and how clean the floors and tables are. Are the plants well watered if you go later in the day?
- **Size does matter!** There are exceptions to every rule, but there are several reasons I recommend buying at least a four inch annual plant:
  - Six-packs or jumbo packs of flowers have smaller root systems because of the size of the container. Planted in a full sun pot where the soil will be well heated when first planted, there is a smaller amount of soil around the roots to insulate and protect them when they are 'uprooted' into their new home! A four inch plant has had a chance to spread its roots out more in a larger volume of soil.

Jumbo Six Pack

Choose Healthy Plants - Size Does Matter! (Continued)

> ‣ This does not mean you have to buy gallon plants (annuals). Typically, these are simply three six-pack plants upsized into a gallon can. Unless they are really well grown, save your money and stick with the 4 inch plants.

> ‣ Usually, a 4 inch plant is four to six weeks older than six-pack plants. Therefore it is more mature and will give you earlier and better growth.
> ‣ Exceptions to my 'No Six-Pack" rule are well grown alyssum, lobelia and other small leafed plants or lettuces and herbs. Well-grown means the top and the roots are sizable.

◉ Characteristics

> ‣ **Foliage -** Are the leaves bright, clean and lush? Avoid any plants with many yellow leaves or a plant that is wilting. Plants that are showing these kinds of stress may not recover and are more susceptible to pests and disease.

- **Shape** - Unless you are looking at trees or structural plants with a single stem or trunk, you want to cue in on plants that have multiple stems and a compact, full shape. Plants with spindly, weak stems and branches are not the best to buy.
- **Flowers** - Choose flowering plants with a large number of buds. A budding plant will give you more

immediate gratification than one that has many open flowers that will need to be deadheaded soon. Many experts will suggest deflowering the plant before planting it but I rarely do that. I want my garden to look great as soon as I finish planting it!

- **Insects & Disease** - Inspect closely for signs of insects or disease. Check both sides of the leaves and the potting soil. Signs can include: black or rust colored spots, holes, mushy stems or any stickiness on the leaves. Avoid these like the plague!
- **Root System -** Do not neglect the roots. If the plant is pot bound and the roots are growing out of the bottom, the plant may be stressed and take time to recover. If there aren't many roots and the plant lifts out very easily bringing only loose soil, it was

probably recently repotted and could use more time to become garden worthy. It's perfectly appropriate to gently ease a plant out of the container to look at the roots while at the nursery.

Choose Healthy Plants (Continued)

If you cannot resist the prices offered by a big box store, try to buy them on or close to the day they are delivered. Do not be shy to ask someone who works there which day new plant stock arrives. Delivery is usually the same day every week.

> To summarize, remember to look for three things when purchasing plants:
> 1. Top appearance (tight buds, healthy leaves)
> 2. Bushy appearance (well branched and filled out)
> 3. Root appearance (healthy roots that hold soil without being root-bound)

Drought Tolerant - What Does That Mean?

- Drought tolerant landscaping and plants are able to grow or thrive with minimal water or rainfall. Be aware that the terms drought resistant and drought tolerant mean different things. Plants that can survive for long periods of time without water are drought resistant. In others words, they take drought tolerance one step further. For example, a Beaucarnea recurvata (Ponytail Palm) stores water in the bulbous base of its trunk, and once established, can survive for long periods without water.

Drought Tolerant (Continued)

◉ Xeriscape and xeriscaping are terms used to describe a landscaping style that uses drought-tolerant plants to help conserve water.

Full Size vs. Dwarf Trees

◉ Most plants are automatically reduced in their growing size because their roots are "contained." Since they are unable to spread out in open spaces, they do keep their branches more in line with the size of the root volume. There are always exceptions to this 'rule' and you will discover that some plants just keep growing and growing.

◉ Dwarf fruit trees are created by grafting a fruit variety onto a dwarf rootstock. Planted in the ground, they will only grow 8-12' tall. In containers, they will be smaller but they will continue to grow and will need to be repotted into larger containers and may need to also be root pruned. My next book will include a section on growing trees in pots.

Evergreen vs. Deciduous

- Evergreen plants keep their leaves throughout the year.
- Deciduous plants lose their leaves seasonally and some varieties need to be cut back.
- Semi-deciduous plants typically lose their leaves at the same time they are growing new ones. In mild winters, this will seem like a minor shedding of old leaves.

Frost Tender Plants

- Frost tender plants will be damaged or killed in temperatures where frost or freezing occurs. In the desert, if a plant is labeled frost tender, it can be sensitive at temperatures as high as 45 degrees but definitely will be affected when the mercury goes to 35 or below.

PLANTING FOR SUCCESS

Be Prepared

If you now have your pots, placement, soil and plant list ready, it's time to go shopping! Be sure to consider timing. Shopping can be time consuming, so don't plan to do too much in one day because once the plants are purchased, you want to have allocated enough time to plant as soon as possible.

Remember, the sun moves, so be sure the plants remain in the shade and if temperatures are above 70°, water them thoroughly to make sure that the plants don't dry out prior to planting.

Double check that your pots have good drainage. A hole of at least one inch is needed in each pot. Check before you buy them. A good nursery or pot shop will be able to drill the holes for you.

Pot Placement and Prep

- If possible, place your pot in the spot you want it to remain permanently.
- Cover the drainage hole(s) with screening or a folded coffee filter for the water to drain through. Do not use pot shards or rocks.

Pot Placement and Prep (Continued)

- If you want to seal the inside of the pot, use a product such as DRYLOK®, a masonry waterproofing product found in the paint department of most hardware stores. Pots that are glazed on the inside do not need to be sealed.
- Fill pot with soil. Depending on the size of the pot, stop filling each 12 to18 inches and compress the soil with your hands to pack it down "nicely." Take care not to pack the soil so intensely there will not be any air left in the soil. Air pockets will cause the water to flow through, dropping the top soil level.
- Unless you are planting 1 gallon containers or larger, bring the soil up to 2 inches from the top of the pot. When planting larger plants, do not fill as full so that you can first get the plant in and then continue to add soil.
- Add time-release fertilizer to the soil. Follow the directions on the container or use a small handful for each 18" of pot size. Distribute the fertilizer throughout the top 2" of soil depth. You do not need to worry about mixing it in beyond this as ongoing watering will continue to deliver the food down throughout the root structure.

Prepping Your Plants

- In the warmer months, make sure root balls on plants are damp before planting. If they are dry, take a pail of water and hold the entire can (not plant) under water until bubbles stop coming out of the soil.

Prepping Your Plants (Continued)

- Remove the plant from the container by tipping the plant onto its side, squish the pot to loosen the root ball and gently ease the plant out. DO NOT pull the plant by its stem or trunk as you may damage it and risk killing the plant.

- If all or part of the root ball is gray, it means it is not thoroughly watered. Slip it back into the can and submerge in water as explained above.

- Tickle the roots - well - not exactly. Well-rooted plants can be loosened by grabbing each side and easing apart. Yes, some of the roots will tear and that is what you want so they are encouraged to branch out into their new home. If the plant is lightly rooted, be gentle and tickle them apart.

Planting

- Dig a hole the size of the root ball and place the plant into it. Press it down gently and add soil around the plant. Do not add soil any higher than it was in the container as it will suffocate the top of the tender air roots that are close to the surface.
- Push down on your plants to finish seating them in the soil.
- Add the next plants, keeping them about an inch apart, shoulder to shoulder.
- Even if the plants were moist before planting, water the entire pot well when planting is complete. You should see water coming out of the drainage hole.
- Water sun pots every day unless they are sufficiently wet the next morning. During these first two weeks, it is crucial to not let the roots dry out. Remember, because they are near the top two inches of soil they are more likely to dry out quickly in the desert heat and wind.

Make sure that your plants have all the requirements they need: **food, water and oxygen.**

The First Two Weeks After Planting Your 'Soft' Plants
- New plantings must be well watered. Having just come from the nursery where in the summer months they might have been watered four times a day, they are used to being wet. For the first two weeks maintain a vigorous watering schedule. Then once you see good growth, pull back to normal watering.

Ongoing Care

Being Mindful! I want you to enjoy your new container gardens but be mindful of surrounding conditions and try to head off any problems before they happen.
- Check Irrigation. If your pots are on an irrigation system, make sure it is running and all the emitters are working. If something is looking sad, investigate and see if you can find out why. Is the line getting clogged because water is not draining out properly? Did a pet or other creature bite a hole in the line or pull it out? Did the system get turned off? No need to check these things every day but by being mindful and in tune with your plants, you will always ensure a successful garden!

Ongoing Care (Continued)

- **Fertilizing.** After about two weeks or when you start seeing new growth in your pots, it's time to begin a regular fertilizing program. Because watering daily flushes out nutrients, you should feed your plants every two weeks.

  ‣ Use a water soluble fertilizer (Miracle Grow® is a good example but certainly not the only product out there). Water soluble fertilizers need to be diluted in water. You can mix it in a bucket or watering can but I recommend using a sprayer that attaches to your hose. It is a time-saver and you can 'foliar feed" the leaves at the same time you are feeding the plant.

  ‣ Apply enough of the solution so that you see water coming out of the drainage holes. You want to apply it to the entire root ball and pot circumference.

  ‣ DO NOT apply the powder directly to the plant and then water it in. It is too concentrated and will burn/kill the plant.

  ‣ Each time you pot up a container, add a time-release fertilizer to the soil.

Ongoing Care (Continued)

◉ **Blasting Your Plants**. Many people shudder when I suggest you blast plants with a jet spray of your hose. But, this is the first method of defense against pests and disease. It not only knocks things off the leaves but it

also aerates the plants. This is great for potted gardens where the plants are arranged close together and can this extra burst of oxygen.

  ▸ Standing about 4 feet away from plants, set the nozzle on your hose to jet spray, and let 'er rip!

  ▸ Do this in the morning so they have a chance to dry out during the day. Don't worry about water on the leaves, the sun will not burn them.

◉ **Deadheading.** Any plant that flowers is going to give more prolific blooms if you deadhead (remove the dead flowers). It not only improves the look of plants but also encourages growth and prolongs life.

  ▸ When a flowering plant blooms and is not deadheaded regularly, it will create seeds (procreate), sending energy to the dead flowers as if its life is over and will begin the dying process.

  ▸ Using pruners, scissors or your fingers, clip the bloom and its stem all the way back to where it originated on the plant or even further back towards the center of the plant where you see baby leaves. This will make the plant bushier.

Ongoing Care (Continued)

- **Pruning.** It's time to prune when potted plants start looking leggy or ragged. With a good "haircut," they will come back healthier and happier. On many flowering plants, if you prune them regularly throughout the season, you will never lose the look and beauty of the plant.
Plan your cuts deep within the plant rather than pruning the outer most branches or stems. This will create a fuller plant, not one that is spindly.

  > Take petunias or snapdragons for example - Unpruned, they get leggy or very tall and don't have a chance to bush out. Vinca, a summer plant, will also get very long and as temperatures begin to cool, older leaves and stems will start yellowing while new growth from within the plant is just waiting to be set free.

- The process noted above is selective pruning. To reiterate, about six to eight weeks after planting, prune any long branches back to new growth in the center of the plant. Looking at your entire plant, select branches to prune throughout the plant, taking 1/3 of the plant at a time. Continue this process every two weeks around the entire plant for the next month and your plant will be full and robust.

Cutting Point

Ongoing Care (Continued)

- ◉ **Do Not Over Water.** Our tendency is to love our plants to death. To avoid over-watering your container gardens:
  - ‣ Make sure your pots have adequate drainage holes.
  - ‣ Know the moisture requirements for your plants.
  - ‣ Before you water, check the soil with a moisture meter or a pencil, placing it into the soil to the level of the roots. A meter has a reading while a pencil will come out with clumping soil particles if damp.
  - ‣ For most annuals and soft perennials, water when it is dry within the top two inches.
  - ‣ For cacti, succulents and drought tolerant plants, water when the root level is dry.

- ◉ **Signs of Overwatering:**
  - ‣ Leaves turn yellow and fall off.
  - ‣ Limp plants – sometimes lack of water and too much water can make the plant look droopy – to be sure which it is, check the soil for moisture!

- ◉ **Do Not Under-Water.** Most container gardens need watering at least once a day in the heat of the summer. Many, especially hanging planters or small containers need watering even more often because there is less soil to retain the moisture.

- ◉ When you water, make sure to really soak your plants. If you just give them a sip, the water will only wet the top layer of soil. Water until it begins to run out the bottom of the pot.

Ongoing Care - Do Not Under-Water (Continued)

- If plants dry out, most will revive with a good, timely drink. If the container is small enough, submerge the entire pot in a bucket of water until the air bubbles subside. For a large container, water thoroughly (until water drains through the bottom) and water again 30 minutes later.

Parting Thoughts: Better Dirt than Dead

After you have tried everything, and your plant still looks like a lost cause, cut your losses and toss it on the compost pile. If only one plant in your container garden is dead, remove that plant and replace it.

If you have a full pot of dead plants, you should investigate the cause. Did the pot not have enough water? Is there a pest or disease problem? Before replanting, resolve the issue. If the soil or disease is suspect, dispose of the soil and sterilize the pot with a 10% solution of bleach, rinse and dry thoroughly.

If you are the type of gardener who cannot stand to throw away a plant that has a bit of life left, put it in your plant nursery to see if you can bring it back to life. This way, you are only looking at it when you choose to!

APPENDIX

Flowers & Colorful Leaf Plants for Desert Potted Gardens - Master Plant Lists by Season

Planting Guide by Season

Fertilizing Instructions & Schedule for Annuals

Watering Guide

Weather Maps/Zones

Inside Plants > Outside

Javelina & Critter Resistance

Online Link for Resources
www.potteddesert.com/GettingPottedResources

FLOWERS & COLORFUL LEAF PLANTS FOR DESERT POTTED GARDENS

Master Plant List by Season

- ◉ Many of the plants listed are perennials that are often treated as annuals as they do not do well in the other seasons.
- ◉ Red or BOLD indicates low water plants.
- ◉ *This list has been developed by Marylee Pangman for The Potted Desert. Do not reproduce without permission. (All Rights Reserved).*

Winter

Flower	Comments
African Daisy (Osteospermum)	Will not bloom much when cold; Shoulder Season
Ageratum	
Alyssum	Fragrant; Attracts butterflies
Arctotis (African Daisy Family)	Will not grow during cold months
Calendula	Edible flowers in orange and yellow
Candytuft	Attracts butterflies
Carnation (Dianthus family)	Blooms less in cold; Shoulder Season Plant; Attracts butterflies
Cordyline	Shade; Frost Tender; Stature plant
Cyclamen	Shade
Delphinium	Late winter
Diascia	Lesser known annual with small but ample flowers
Dianthus (look for *Amazon* and other tall varieties for height)	Blooms less in cold; Shoulder Season; Attracts butterflies

Winter (Continued)

Dusty Miller	Gray leafed plant for contrast; Shoulder Season
Foxglove	Late winter
Geranium	Frost tender; Shoulder Season
Gerbera Daisies	Afternoon shade; Shoulder Season
Heuchera (Coral Bells)	Shade
Hollyhock	Late winter
Kalenchoe	Shade – Frost Tender
Larkspur	Late winter
Lobelia	Frost tender; will do well in some shade
Nasturtiums	Fragrant
Nemesia	Lesser known annual with nice array of colors
Ornamental Cabbage	Beautiful leaf patterns, new varieties every year
Osteospermum	African Daisy; Shoulder Season
Pansy	Old reliable, very cold hardy
Petunia	Blooms less in cold; Shoulder Season Flower; Selective pruning to new growth recommended for longevity
Poppy	Iceland variety
Primrose (Primula; English Primrose)	Shade
Ranunculus	Afternoon shade; Late winter/early spring
Schizanthus	Be sure to ask for this winner!
Snapdragons	Blooms less in cold; Shoulder Season Plant; Consistently prune stems back to new growth for a full plant.
Stock	Fragrant
Sweet Peas	Fragrant
Viola	Will do well in some shade

Master Plant List by Season

Summer

Flower - Sun	Comments
Angelonia (Summer Snap Dragon)	Responds well to late-season pruning
Artemisias	Perennial; many great varieties; Selective pruning to new growth recommended for longevity
Arctotis (African Daisy)	Shoulder season tall daisy like flower, Perennial, cut back to stimulate new growth
Brachyscome	Smaller daisy like flower similar to Arctotis, petals more narrow, from Australia
Calibrachoa (Million Bells)	Small trailing petunia shaped flower with bold colors and bi-color selections
Canna	Tropical lily like flower, huge leaves, wind damage likely
Carex (grass like)	Perennial that rarely needs cutting back
Celosia	Beautiful brilliant plume flowers, some take the heat better than others, ask for recommendations at your local nursery.
Coreopsis	Attracts butterflies
Cosmos - protected	Cut back when tired, surround with other annuals; will bounce back in fall
Cuphea	Frost tender Perennial; Needs lots of water
Diascia – morning sun only	See winter
Diamond Frost	Another Euphorbia, surprise tiny flower that rises above your lower plants
Dusty Miller	Perennial
Dysodia	Smelly small yellow daisy flower but works against critters
Evolvulus	Perennial
Euphorbia – Protected	Huge family of plants, surprising features, talk to your nursery

Summer (Continued)

Gallardia	"Blanket" flower related to sunflowers; medium tall plants
Gaura	Perennial
Gazania	Perennial; Will only bloom while the sun is on the plant
Gomphrena	Many great varieties
Grasses	Look for those you don't need to cut back in winter. Sedge family
Hibiscus	Morning sun; frost tender
Ipomoea (Sweet Potato "vine")	Many new varieties/colors; long vining leafy plant, will wilt in afternoon heat but rebound in the morning; dies back in frost
Lantana	Perennial; Attracts butterflies, freezes back in winter
Lavenders	Perennial; Do NOT overwater
Nemesia - morning sun only	See winter
Nicotiana	Afternoon shade is best
Nierembergia	Responds well to pruning
Osteospermum	Shoulder season flowering plant, daisy like flowers, "African Daisy"
Pentas	Great full sun summer bloomer
Petunia	In cooler regions
Phlox	Attracts butterflies
Portulaca	Moss Rose; If this gets sad looking, reduce water; Attracts butterflies
Purslane	Will only bloom while the sun is on the plant
Rudbeckia	Attracts butterflies
Salvia: Annual	Attracts butterflies
Salvia: Perennial	Attracts butterflies

Summer (Continued)

Scabiosa	Perennial; Somewhat invasive so watch for volunteers
Scaevola	Great full sun summer trailing bloomer
Verbena: Annual	Selective pruning to new growth recommended for longevity
Verbena: Perennial	Selective pruning to new growth recommended for longevity; Attracts butterflies
Vinca	Selective pruning to new growth recommended for longevity
Wallflower	Perennial; Attracts butterflies
Zinnia	All types DO NOT LET DRY OUT; Profusion variety responds well to pruning; Attracts butterflies.
Shade	
Ajuga	Showy low growing leaf plant for shade pots
Begonia	Best in shade, long living if not hit by freeze; prune as needed
Coleus	Many can go in the sun but tend to wash out in Tucson; Selective pruning to new growth recommended for longevity; Do not allow to flower
Dichondra	Green or gray leaves
Heliotrope	Nice deep purple flower; Attracts butterflies
Heuchera	Low growing leafy plant with small flowers on long upright stems
Hypoestes	Polka Dot Plant
Iresine	Frost tender, colorful foliage
Impatiens	Frost tender; prune to stimulate new growth
Lamium	Frost tender, great silver leaf color
Oxalis	Challenging
Sedums	All types some can even go in the sun but they change colors with direct sunlight.

Master Plant List by Season
Edible Flowers

Summer	Winter
Basil	Calendula
Chamomile	Herb flowers
Lavender	Lavender
Okra	Nasturtiums
Purslane	Pansies
Salvia	Violas
Roses	
Daylilies	
Begonia	
Squash blossoms	
Dianthus	
Marigold	

Favorite Vines

Vine	Comments
Bower Vine	Morning sun
Cape Honeysuckle	Hummingbirds
Caroline Jasmine	Yellow Flowers
Cat's Claw	Beware: Attaches to wall
Honeysuckle	Hummingbirds
Jasmine – Confederate	Some sun
Lilac Vine	Purple flowers with a chartreuse center spot; remind me of small Wisteria flowers
Potato Vine	Tender perennial vine
Star Jasmine	Shade
Tangerine Beauty X-Vine	A favorite of MP; Hummingbirds
Yellow trumpet vine	Hummingbirds

Rabbit, Javelina & Deer Resistant Plants

Because of drought conditions over the past few years, desert critters like javelina, deer and rabbits are looking at our plants as food and water sources. Plants with tubular roots and vegetable plantings are particularly attractive to them. Squirrels and birds are also troublesome and can damage plants. I have yet to find definitive solutions to these problems.

There is no guarantee for the following methods, so experiment with different options and cross your fingers! The best methods to protect your pots are:

- Don't plant salad type plants and flowers in areas with easy access to animals. This includes flowers like pansies!

- Plant smelly plants and flowers like Sage, Artemesia, and Dahlberg Daisies (see the list below for other plants that can be used)
- Use tall pots with wide bases so they cannot tip over.
- Rim the pot with trailing rosemary to deter exploring noses.
- Fencing, solid walls and closed gates are your best offense in the world of desert critters.

These are plants that are less likely to be eaten by javelina but there are no guarantees that they won't touch them. The only effective measure is a barrier/fencing strong enough to exclude the javelina.

Agave	Arizona Yellow Bell
Aloe	Artemesia
Alyssum (Allysum spp.)	Aster
Angelonia	Autumn Sage

Rabbit, Javelina & Deer Resistant Plants (Continued)
Common Name (Botanical Name)

Basil (Ocimum spp.)
Black Dalea
Blanketflower (Gaillardia)
Brittlebush !!
Butterfly Bush (Buddleia spp.)
Cape Honeysuckles
Carnations (Dianthus spp.)
Chaste Tree (Vitex)
Chili Pepper (Capsicum Annuum)
Chrysanthemum
(Chrysanthemum spp.)
Chuparosa
Cosmos (Cosmso spp.)
Cucumbers (Cucumis sativus)
Daffodils (Narcissus spp.)
Dahlberg Daisy
Daylily (Hemerocallis spp.)
Deerbrush (Ceanothus spp.)
Desert Marigold
Desert Milkweed
Desert Spoon
Dicliptera
Dusty Miller
Easter Lily
(Lillium Longiflorum)
Eggplant (Solanum Melogena)
Emu Bush
Euphorbia Family
(due to the bitter milky substance inside)
Fairy Duster
Cassia Feathery !!

Gazania
Geraniums (Geranium spp.)
Globe Amaranth (Gomphrena spp.)
Golden Fleece
Gomphrena
Hen & Chicks (Echeveria Elegans)
Hesperaloe
Hibiscus (Hibiscus spp.)
Hummingbird Bush
Ice Plant (Mesembryanthemum spp.)
Indian Mallow
Iris (Iris spp.)
Ivy (Hedera spp.)
Justicia spicigera
(also known as Mexican honeysuckle)
Lambs Ear
Lantana

!! = Plants Not Recommended
to Grow in Pots

Rabbit, Javelina & Deer Resistant Plants (Continued)
Common Name (Botanical Name)

Larkspur (Delphinium spp.)
Lavandula 'Purple Ribbon'
Lilac (Syringa spp)
Little Leaf Cordial
Manzanita (Arctostaphylos spp.)
Marigolds (Tagetes spp.)
Mexican Bird of Paradise !!
Mexican Oregano
Pampas Grass !! (Cortaderia Selloana)
Plumbago
Petunias (Petunia Hybrida)
Plumbago
Portulaca (Portulaca Grandiflora)
Prairie Zinnia
Queen's Wreath
Red-Hot Poker (Kniphofia Uvaria)
Rose Bushes (Rosa spp.)

Ruellia Peninsularis (Desert Ruellia)
Russian Sage
Sage (Salvia officinalis)
Salvia Clevelandii (Cleveland Cage)
Squash
Santolina (Santolina)
Snapdragons (Antirrhinum Majus)
Sweet William (Dianthus Barbatus)
Texas Mescal Bean
(also called Texas Mountain Laurel)
Texas Ranger
(also known as Texas sage) !!
Trailing iIndigo Bush
Verbena
Vinca
Yucca

!! = Plants Not Recommended to Grow in Pots

PLANTING GUIDE BY SEASON

Nighttime Temperatures are Key		
True Winter	November – March	Plant winter flowers when nights are in the 50's
Shoulder Season Spring	March – Late April	
True Summer	May – Late September	Plant summer flowers when nights are in the 60's
Shoulder Season Fall	September – Mid October	

Shoulder Seasons are those in-between seasons when strong winter or summer flowers are not typically available. Even if some nurseries bring in winter or summer flowers, they should not be planted in pots until the night time temperatures reach those listed above. Patience is needed here because we are often chomping at the bit to go ahead and plant. Flowers listed as shoulder season flowers will do well in the short seasons listed above.

My favorite shoulder season flowers are:

- Petunias
- Dianthus
- Snapdragons
- Marigolds
- Dusty Miller (for contrasting leaf color)
- Geraniums

FERTILIZING INSTRUCTIONS & SCHEDULE FOR ANNUALS

	Product	Frequency	Comments
Initial Planting	Time release fertilizer found in all nurseries.	Each seasonal planting; more often for citrus (see Month by Month Guide)	Use approximately one handful for every 18" of pot diameter. Sprinkle around soil before planting. As you add plants the fertilizer will mix into the soil. Be sure, as always, to water your pot thoroughly after planting.
Beginning about 2 weeks after planting; when you see new growth on the plants	Water Soluble Fertilizer	Every two weeks	Best if applied with a hose attachment canister found in the nursery. One canister of fertilizer will feed about 40 XL pots. Shower the plant and the entire soil surface until water drains out of the pot hole.

WEATHER MAPS | ZONES

- Because microclimates can be cooler or warmer than reported temperatures in your zone, it's a good idea to track air temperatures and average lows throughout the winter in your specific garden to get an idea of what to really expect when chilly weather is forecasted.
- See Resource Link for more information.

WATERING CHART

	Summer Sun	Summer Shade		Winter Shade
Length of Time	5- 15 Minutes	3 - 10 Minutes	5 - 15 Minutes	3- 10 Minutes
Frequency Week 1 & 2	2 x's /Day	Every 1 -2 Days	2 x's /Day	Every 1 -2 Days
Frequency Week 3 & On	1 -2 x's /Day	Every 1 -2 Days	Every 1 -2 Days	Every 2 - 4 Days

- Adjust for temperature changes, individual location needs and monsoon.
- Monitor plants carefully - especially after initial installation
- <u>Only</u> if it rains at least ½" within one hour, can you can forgo watering your container gardens that same day.

INSIDE PLANTS > OUTSIDE

3 Tips on Houseplants

- Provide them with a 'summer vacation' by putting them out on your shaded patio after all danger of frost is past.
- Do not overwater. If you have black flies from your indoor (or shade) plants, the only way to eliminate them is to break their cycle by not watering as often. Use a water meter to see when the soil in the root zone is almost dry. Then drench thoroughly. I water my house plants every three to four weeks!
- Use a houseplant fertilizer ¼ strength every time you water.

ABOUT THE AUTHOR

Marylee Pangman had always dreamed of opening her own business and explored many options but could not find one that fit her goals and talents. Over time, as she gained experience in creating potted gardens in her own desert home and then went on to become a certified Master Gardener, the seeds were planted that grew into "The Contained Gardener", her very own company in the mid-desert of Tucson, AZ.

With her strong vision and goals for success, The Contained Gardener became the standard for exceptional potted landscape design, unparalleled creativity and quality in Southern Arizona's desert community.

The concept for "Get Potted in the Desert." came from Marylee's desire to share the extensive knowledge gained during her 20 years of container gardening through scorching desert summers, annual desert frosts and everything in between.

In our challenging desert climate, Marylee sees container gardening as the ideal way to fulfill our desire to surround desert dwellers with year round living color.

Continue your container gardening success by signing up for the exclusive *I Got Potted* email list. Members receive:

Advanced information on all things potted
Plus Additional:

- ➤ Care recommendations
- ➤ Pictures with all plants listed
- ➤ Plant listings for each month's pictures

Sign up Today!
thepotteddesert.com/free-link/

Made in United States
Orlando, FL
04 December 2021

11137009R00066